THE SCIENCE OF
NATURAL DISASTERS

THE SCIENCE OF
EARTHQUAKES

Kristi Lew

Cavendish
Square

Published in 2020 by Cavendish Square Publishing, LLC
243 5th Avenue, Suite 136, New York, NY 10016

Library of Congress Cataloging-in-Publication Data

Names: Lew, Kristi, author.
Title: The science of earthquakes / Kristi Lew.
Description: First edition. | New York : Cavendish Square, 2020. |
Series: The science of natural disasters | Audience: Grades 2 to 5.
Identifiers: LCCN 2018057993 (print) | LCCN 2019000499 (ebook) |
ISBN 9781502646453 (ebook) | ISBN 9781502646446 (library bound) |
ISBN 9781502646422 (pbk.) | ISBN 9781502646439 (6 pack)
Subjects: LCSH: Earthquakes--Juvenile literature. | Earthquake prediction--Juvenile literature.
Classification: LCC QE521.3 (ebook) | LCC QE521.3 .L49 2020 (print) | DDC 551.22--dc23
LC record available at https://lccn.loc.gov/2018057993

Editorial Director: David McNamara
Editor: Kristen Susienka
Copy Editor: Nathan Heidelberger
Associate Art Director: Alan Sliwinski
Designer: Ginny Kemmerer
Production Coordinator: Karol Szymczuk
Photo Research: J8 Media

Printed in the United States of America

CONTENTS

An earthquake in Nepal in 2015 caused severe damage to buildings and roads. In fact, it was so strong it moved entire structures!

CHAPTER 1

WHAT IS AN EARTHQUAKE?

The ground shakes. The dishes rattle. A picture on the wall swings and falls. The glass shatters when it hits the floor. What is going on?

People come out of their homes. When they look around, they are shocked and shaken. They see cracks in the walls of their houses. Trees have toppled over. The sidewalk is broken into pieces.

One neighbor calls out, "Was that an earthquake?"

"I think it was," answers another.

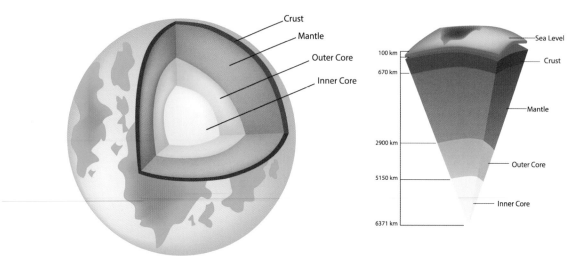

Earth has four major layers. The outer layer is the crust. The crust is thickest under land and thinner under oceans.

The Broken Crust

What is an earthquake? An earthquake is a sudden, strong movement of Earth's surface. The surface of Earth is called its **crust**.

Earth's crust is not solid. It is broken into pieces, called plates. The plates lie on top of the **mantle**. Earth's mantle is made up of hot, liquefied rock. As the liquid rock moves, the plates that make up the crust move with it.

There are eight major plates that make up the crust. They are named for large landforms around them. For example, the Pacific Plate makes up the floor of the Pacific Ocean. The North American plate is the part of the crust on which North America lies. The other major plates are called the Eurasian, African, Indian, Australian, South American, and Antarctic plates.

As the plates of Earth's crust move, they slide under, over, or past each other. Sometimes, the plates get stuck. If this happens, pressure builds as the plates try to move. In the end, the pressure is so much that

DID YOU KNOW?

The plates that make up Earth's crust move about 1 to 2 inches (2 to 5 centimeters) per year. Your fingernails grow at about the same speed.

it breaks the rocks that make up the plate. When that happens, an earthquake forms.

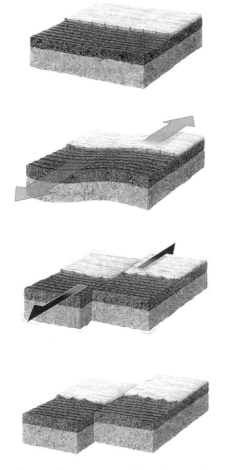

These illustrations show how the plates of Earth's crust move.

Where Do Earthquakes Happen?

Earthquakes can happen when a volcano erupts. Human activities, like exploding a bomb, can cause an earthquake too. However, most earthquakes happen on **faults**. A fault is a crack in Earth's crust where blocks of rock move against each other. The

THE RING OF FIRE

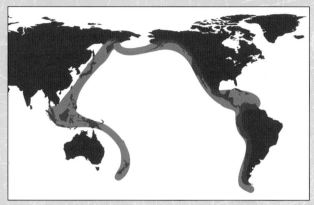

The Ring of Fire traces the edges of the Pacific Plate. Many earthquakes and volcanic eruptions happen here.

The Ring of Fire is a horseshoe-shaped area in the Pacific Ocean. It traces the border of the Pacific Plate. Beginning at the southern tip of South America, the ring stretches up the west coast of the United States to Alaska. It then moves across the Bering Strait, down through Japan, and into New Zealand.

The Ring of Fire is the most active earthquake area in the world. Nearly 90 percent of all the world's earthquakes happen there. Its name comes from the fact that it also has the largest number of active volcanoes in the world.

This photograph shows a tsunami in Japan swallowing cars and homes while people look on.

This is the San Andreas Fault.

places where Earth's plates come together are called fault lines. However, faults can also form in the middle of plates.

The San Andreas Fault is a famous fault. It is in California. It has caused a lot of very powerful earthquakes.

DID YOU KNOW?

If an earthquake happens under the ocean, it can cause another type of natural disaster called a tsunami. A tsunami is a set of giant waves.

Snapping your fingers is an
example of friction at work.

CHAPTER 2

EARTHQUAKE SCIENCE

Two of Earth's plates move past each other at California's San Andreas Fault. The plates do not always slide smoothly. Sometimes, they get stuck. Think about what happens when you snap your fingers. First, you press your fingertips together. Then, you try to slide one finger past the other. At first, a force called **friction** keeps one finger from slipping past the other. Then, suddenly, you press hard enough for friction to be overcome. When that happens, energy is released, or given off. You hear the energy as a sound. Snap!

Earthquake Waves

The same type of thing happens at the San Andreas Fault. Friction keeps the rocks from moving easily. Pressure builds up. Then, suddenly, the rocks break free and energy is released. The energy is released in the form of a wave. In the case of snapping fingers, the energy waves are in the form of sound waves. In the case of an earthquake, the energy waves are called seismic waves.

Seismic waves move through the

When rocks break free, energy is released in the form of seismic waves.

ground. The underground place where an earthquake starts is called its **hypocenter**, or focus. Seismic waves travel outward from the hypocenter. If a straight line is drawn from the hypocenter to Earth's surface, that spot on Earth's crust is the earthquake's **epicenter**. Seismic waves are at their largest at the earthquake's hypocenter. The earthquake is felt the most at its epicenter. People who live near an earthquake's

EARTHQUAKE

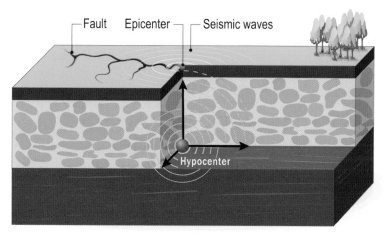

This diagram shows the different parts of an earthquake.

MEASURING EARTHQUAKES

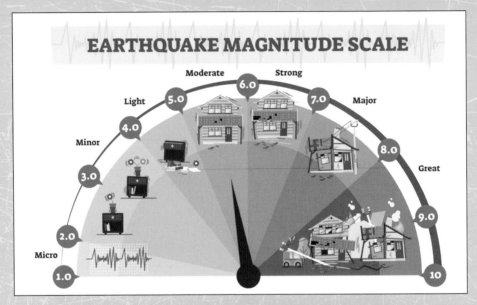

EARTHQUAKE MAGNITUDE SCALE

Micro · 1.0 · 2.0 · 3.0 · Minor · 4.0 · Light · 5.0 · Moderate · 6.0 · Strong · 7.0 · Major · 8.0 · Great · 9.0 · 10

This scale shows the damage each magnitude of earthquake can create. Furniture may move and windows can break during a moderate earthquake. A stronger earthquake can make buildings fall down.

Scientists measure seismic waves using a tool called a seismograph. The size of an earthquake is called its **magnitude**. Scientists report the strength of an earthquake using the moment magnitude scale, or MMS.

The MMS has low numbers and high numbers. Larger earthquakes have higher numbers. People often cannot feel an earthquake that measures below 3.0 on the MMS. However, every increase by a whole number means a ten-fold increase in strength. In other words, a magnitude-7 earthquake is ten times stronger than a magnitude-6. Any earthquake above a 6 is a strong earthquake. Strong earthquakes can damage buildings and cause deaths.

DID YOU KNOW?

The strongest earthquake ever measured had a magnitude of 9.5. It hit Chile in 1960. The largest earthquake in US history had a 9.2 magnitude. It hit Alaska in 1964. In 2018, a 7.0-magnitude quake hit Anchorage, Alaska. Over one thousand aftershocks were recorded in the days after the earthquake. Many buildings and roads were damaged.

epicenter will be the most affected. The farther away from the epicenter you go, the less shaking you will feel.

It Was Such a Shock

Sometimes, the ground shakes before and after a big earthquake. Tremors felt before a large earthquake happens are called foreshocks. Those that happen after are called aftershocks. It is impossible to tell if an earthquake is a foreshock until a bigger earthquake

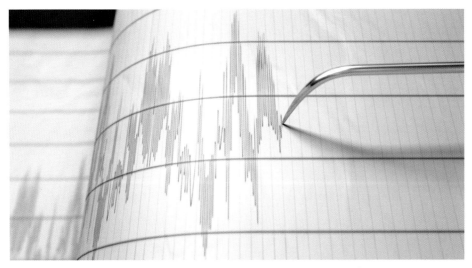

Scientists use a machine called a seismograph to record seismic waves.

comes after it. Sometimes, aftershocks can be felt for hours, days, or even months after the main earthquake has passed.

DID YOU KNOW?

You can make a simple seismograph by punching holes in a box and hanging a pen between them. Then give the table a shake. The pen will record the seismic waves.

Around the world, about half a million earthquakes happen every year. Only about one hundred thousand of those can be felt. The others are too small or too deep inside Earth for people to notice them. Of those that can be felt, only about one hundred of them are strong enough to cause damage.

A car was trapped when the road caved in during an earthquake in Alaska in 2018.

People run from aftershocks following a 7.8-magnitude earthquake in China in 2008.

In the United States, Alaska is the state that gets the most earthquakes. It averages about twenty-four thousand earthquakes a year. One of these will be at least a magnitude-7 earthquake. About every fourteen years or so, Alaska gets a magnitude-8 or higher earthquake. North Dakota and Florida are the states that have the smallest number of earthquakes.

Scientists study data from past earthquakes to learn more about them.

CHAPTER 3

PLANNING FOR AND PREDICTING EARTHQUAKES

It is very hard to know when an earthquake will happen. The best scientists can do is to let people know as soon as possible that an earthquake has started. Seismic waves move at about 2 miles (3.2 kilometers) per second. If scientists detect shock waves from an earthquake, they can let people farther away know that an earthquake is on its way. This can help people prepare for the shaking that will occur.

NEW WAYS TO SENSE AN EARTHQUAKE

Underground fiber-optic cables are helping detect earthquakes.

Scientists and engineers are trying to find new ways to detect seismic waves early. One new tool they are using is fiber-optic cable. These cables are used to carry email and internet traffic from one part of Earth to another. They are also good at sensing seismic waves. These waves jiggle the cables. Larger waves and waves that are closer move the cables more. Using computers, scientists can look at how all the cables jiggle. This can tell scientists where the seismic waves are coming from and how big they are. The cables can help scientists make the earthquake-sensing system larger. More measuring stations can give scientists more information. They can also warn people to get out of harm's way.

Earthquake Engineering

Engineers are also trying to help people in areas where earthquakes happen. They study what happens to buildings and bridges during an earthquake. They make **models** of buildings and bridges. Models are much smaller buildings or bridges made from materials like cardboard or steel. They test their models on a shake table. A shake table moves like the ground does

Scientists use a shake table to compare models of a building. The model on the left is quakeproof. The model on the right is not.

The best place to be during an earthquake is under a sturdy piece of furniture.

during an earthquake. Engineers can then build safer structures.

Actions for an Earthquake

Earthquakes can happen at any time, so it's important to be prepared. The safest place to be is inside. Go where nothing can fall on top of you. Under a large piece of furniture like a table or a desk is perfect.

Before an earthquake hits, choose a safe place in every room of your house. Ask your parents to bolt tall furniture that could topple over. Have them put latches on kitchen cabinets so they don't open and spill what is inside. Finally, put together an emergency kit. A kit can include canned food, bottled water, a charged cell phone, a flashlight, and a battery-run radio with fresh batteries. Simple first-aid items—bandages, tape, and antibiotic cream—are also good to add.

If you're in an earthquake, drop, take cover, and hold on. Protect your eyes and your head. If you are in a building or a car, stay inside until the ground stops shaking. If you are outside, move away from buildings, trees, and power lines.

Stay calm and covered until the shaking stops. It may take some time for the adults around you to check

DID YOU KNOW?

The moon has "earthquakes" too. They are called moonquakes. Moonquakes are usually gentler than earthquakes. They do not happen as often as earthquakes either.

People take part in an earthquake drill at a grocery store in California in 2011.

that the area is safe. Follow their instructions. Once the danger has passed, ask what you can do to help your community get back to normal.

GLOSSARY

crust The outermost layer of Earth; its surface.

epicenter The point on Earth's surface directly above the spot where earthquake waves have started.

fault A crack in Earth's crust.

friction A force that keeps things from moving easily when rubbing against each other.

hypocenter The underground spot where an earthquake begins.

magnitude The size and strength of an earthquake.

mantle The layer of Earth under the crust that is made up of melted rock.

model A smaller version of a structure, like a building or bridge.

FIND OUT MORE

Books

Perish, Patrick. *Survive an Earthquake*. Minneapolis, MN: Bellwether Media, Inc., 2017.

Stark, Kristy. *Predicting Earthquakes*. Huntington Beach, CA: Teacher Created Materials, 2018.

Website

National Geographic Kids: Earthquake

https://kids.nationalgeographic.com/explore/science/earthquake/#earthquake-houses.jpg
Read more about earthquakes at this website.

Video

The Dr. Binocs Show: What Is an Earthquake?

https://www.youtube.com/watch?v=dJpIU1rSOFY
Here, see a seismograph work, learn more about Earth's plates, and view what happens during an earthquake.

INDEX

Page numbers in **boldface** refer to images. Entries in **boldface** are glossary terms.

ABOUT THE AUTHOR

Kristi Lew has written many books for teachers and young people. Fascinated with science from a young age, she studied biochemistry and genetics in college. When she's not writing or reading, she can be found sailing or kayaking around the Gulf of Mexico.